How Does My Home Work?

Rubbish and Recycling

Chris Oxlade

www.raintreepublishers.co.uk
Visit our website to find out more information about Raintree books.

To order:
Phone 0845 6044371
Fax +44 (0) 1865 312263
Email myorders@raintreepublishers.co.uk

Customers from outside the UK please telephone +44 1865 312262

Raintree is an imprint of Capstone Global Library Limited, a company incorporated in England and Wales having its registered office at 7 Pilgrim Street, London, EC4V 6LB – Registered company number: 6695582

Edited by Daniel Nunn, Rebecca Rissman, and Catherine Veitch
Designed by Joanna Hinton-Malivoire
Picture research by Elizabeth Alexander
Production by Alison Parsons
Originated by Capstone Global Library Ltd
Printed and bound in China by Leo Paper Products

ISBN 978 1 406 23768 9
16 15 14 13 12
10 9 8 7 6 5 4 3 2 1

British Library Cataloguing in Publication Data
Oxlade, Chris.
Rubbish and recycling. – (How does my home work?)
363.7'288-dc22
A full catalogue record for this book is available from the British Library.

Acknowledgements
We would like to thank the following for permission to reproduce photographs: © Capstone Publishers p. 23 (Karon Dubke); Alamy p. 18 (© Realimage); Corbis p. 11 (© Image Source); Getty Images p. 21 (Will Heap/Dorling Kindersley); iStockphoto pp. 5 (© Dori OConnell), 15 (© BanksPhotos), 23 (© BanksPhotos); Photolibrary pp. 4 (Corbis), 12 (Jochen Tack/Imagebroker.net); Shutterstock pp. 6 (© Adisa), 7 (© David W. Leindecker), 8 (© HomeStudio), 9 (© tkemot), 10 (© Morgan Lane Photography), 13 (© Tomo Jesenicnik), 14 (© Picsfive), 17 (© Rehan Qureshi), 19 (© Evgeny Karandaev), 19 (© Givaga), 20 (© Jaimie Duplass), 23 (© Tomo Jesenicnik), 23 (© Morgan Lane Photography), 23 (© mikeledray); www.recyclenow.com p. 16

Cover photograph of a recycle sign on a recycle bin reproduced with permission of Alamy (© Peter Carroll). Background photograph of plastic bottles reproduced with permission of Shutterstock (© alterfalter).

Back cover photographs of (left) a rubbish tip reproduced with permission of Shutterstock (© Picsfive), and (right) a bin lorry reproduced with permission of Shutterstock (© Tomo Jesenicnik).

Every effort has been made to contact copyright holders of material reproduced in this book. Any omissions will be rectified in subsequent printings if notice is given to the publisher.

We would like to thank Paul Mocroft for his invaluable help in the preparation of this book.

Contents

Some words are shown in bold, **like this**. You can find them in the glossary on page 23.

What is rubbish?

Rubbish is all the stuff we do not want in our homes anymore.

Bags and boxes that things are wrapped in are one type of rubbish.

The food we do not eat is rubbish.

Vegetable peelings and empty cans
are rubbish, too.

What is wrong with rubbish?

Rubbish makes a mess if people do not throw it in a bin.

It spoils the countryside and our streets.

Some rubbish has harmful materials in it, which can harm or kill animals.

Sometimes animals can get trapped by rubbish.

What materials are in rubbish?

The rubbish from our homes contains different materials.

The paper and card in this photograph are from old food packets.

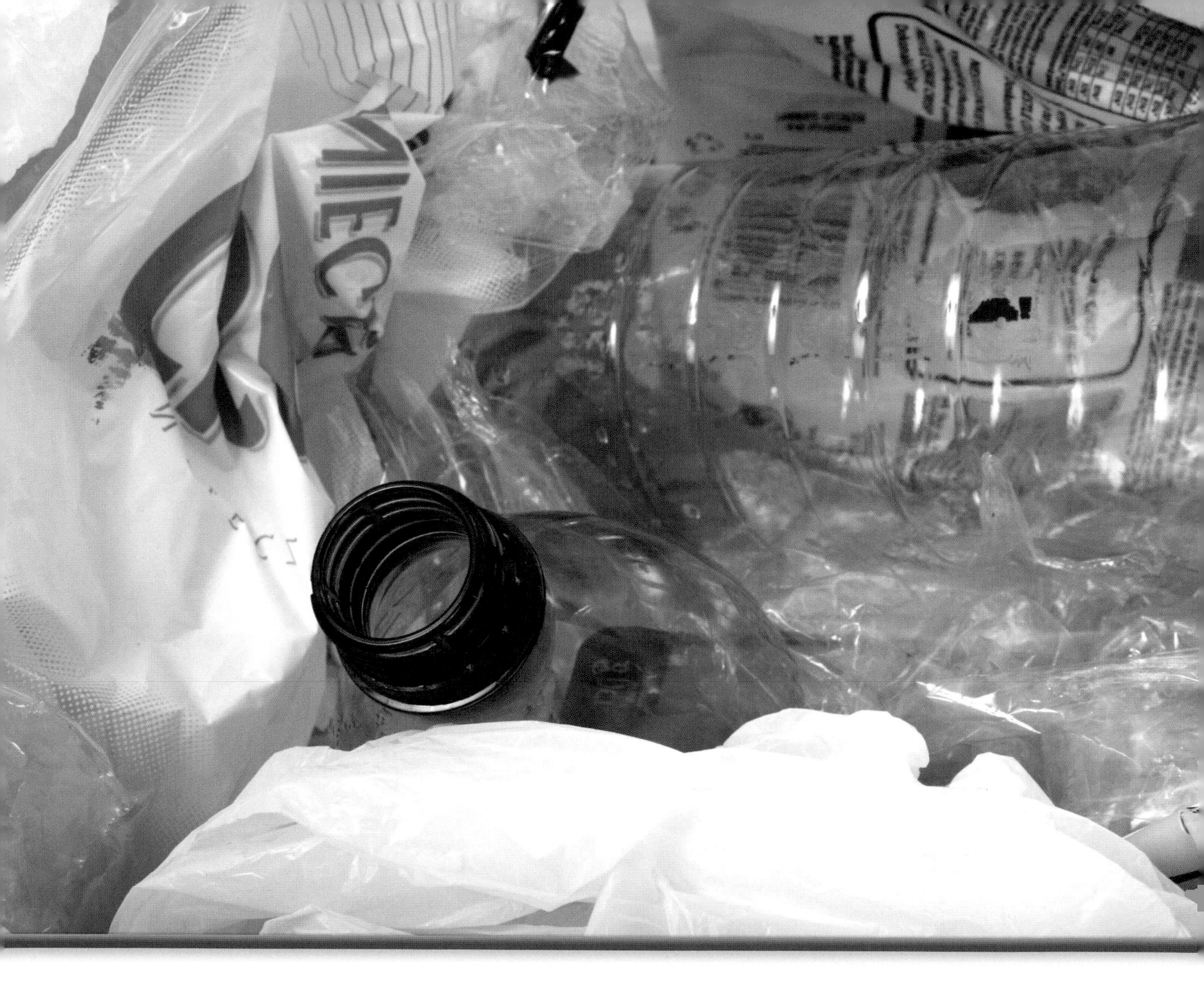

Plastic rubbish comes from plastic bags, bottles, and food containers.

Other materials found in rubbish are glass, metal, food, and garden waste.

Why do we have separate bins for some rubbish?

We can **recycle** paper, card, glass, food cans, and some kinds of plastic.

Recycling means turning rubbish into something new that we can use again.

This bin is for any rubbish that we cannot recycle.

We put things such as nappies and food containers we cannot clean in this bin.

What happens to rubbish after it is taken away?

Bin lorries collect rubbish and recycling materials from our homes.

The lorries also take materials from recycling bins to a **recycling centre**.

Rubbish that cannot be **recycled** is put into a big hole in the ground.

The place where the rubbish is buried is called a **landfill site** or a rubbish tip.

Why don't we bury all our rubbish?

Burying rubbish uses up land.

Burying all our rubbish also wastes materials that we could **recycle**.

Some rubbish is burned instead of being buried.

It is put onto a giant fire inside a container called an **incinerator**.

Why do we recycle materials?

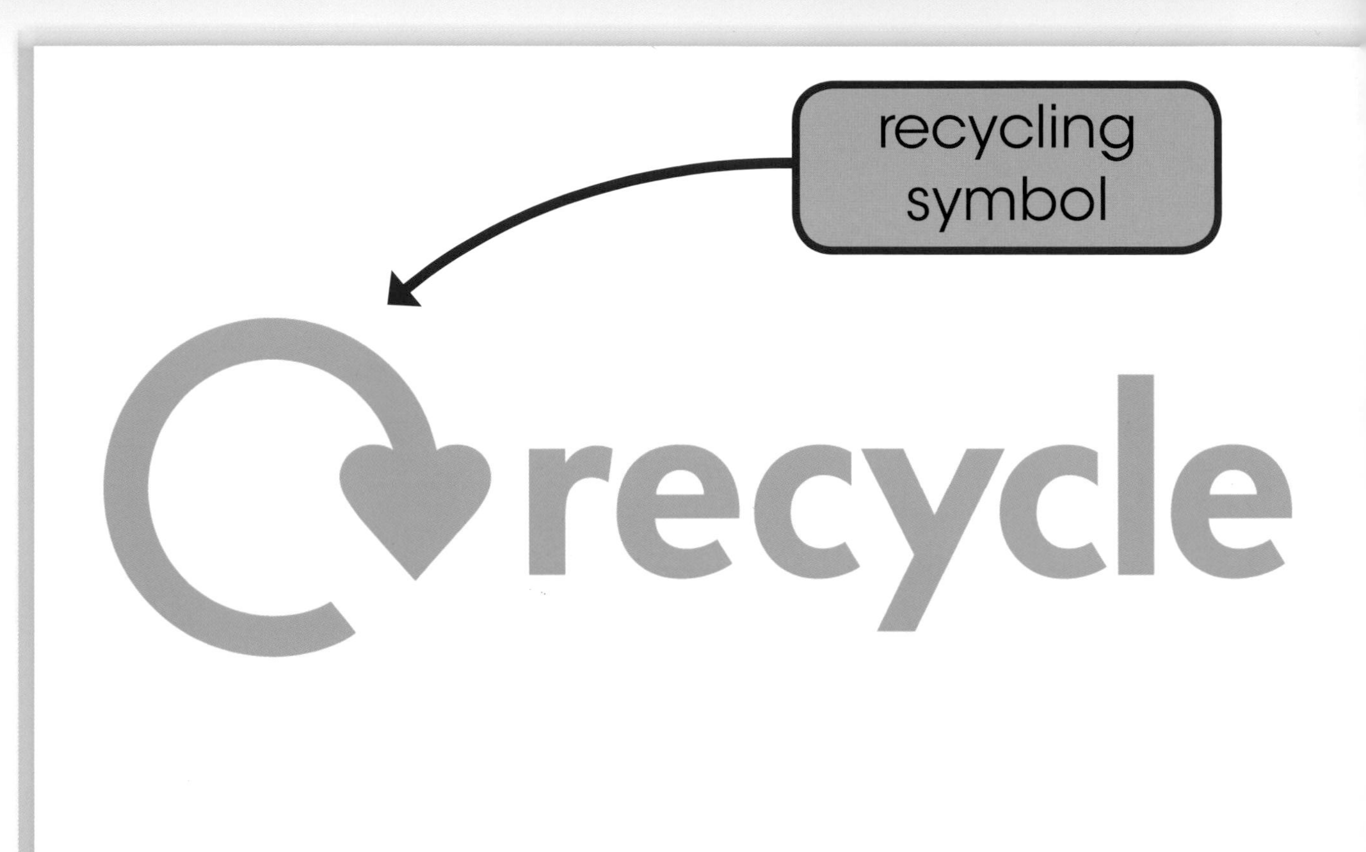

Recycling means that not so much rubbish is buried in **landfill sites**.

When you see this sign, it tells you the material can be **recycled**.

This girl's top is made from recycled material.

Making things from recycled materials means we can use fewer new materials.

How much rubbish do we throw away?

Each day, a person in the United Kingdom throws away about 2 kilograms of rubbish.

That is as heavy as a child's metal scooter!

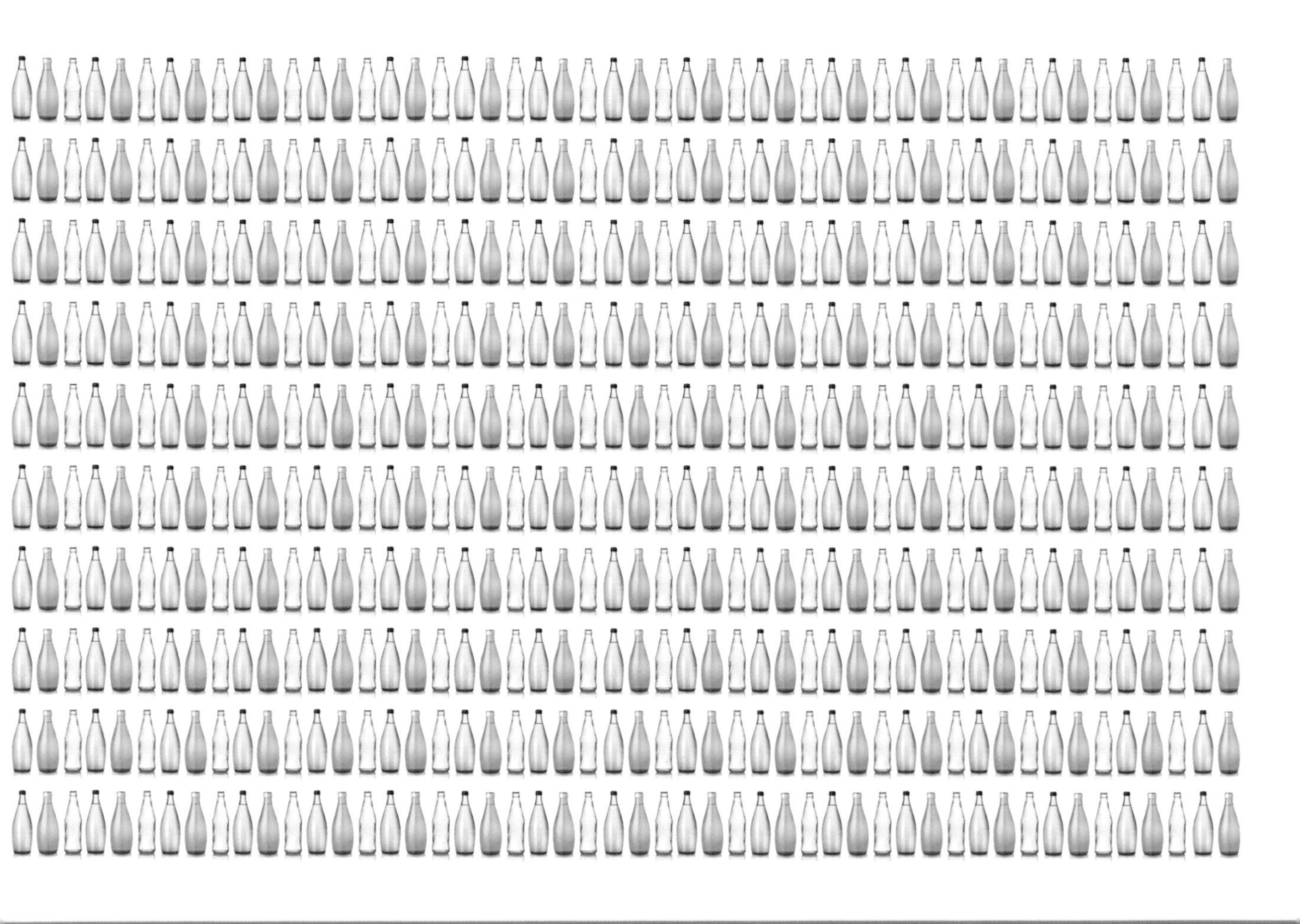

Every year, a family of 4 people throws away about 500 glass bottles and jars.

They also throw away about 1,000 cans and 400 plastic bags.

How can we throw away less?

Stop! Do not throw things that can be **recycled** into a normal rubbish bin.

Put them aside to be collected, or take them to your local **recycling centre**.

You can also **reuse** some things instead of throwing them away.

Yoghurt pots make good plant pots!

Make a recycling tally

How much rubbish does your family **recycle** in a week? List the items below. Then, ask your family to make a **tally** mark each time they put an object in the recycling bin.

Recycling tally

- Glass bottles and jars 𝍸 III
- Plastic bottles III
- Food cans 𝍸 I
- Newspapers/magazines 𝍸 𝍸 II

Glossary

incinerator container or building that holds a fire for burning rubbish

landfill site place where rubbish is buried underground

recycle turn rubbish into something new that can be used again

recycling centre place where you can take materials to be recycled

reuse use a thing again instead of throwing it away

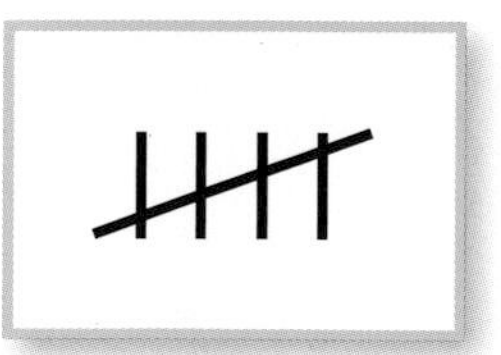

tally record kept so that you can work out the total of something

Find out more

Books

Paper (Reduce, Reuse, Recycle), Alexandra Fix (Heinemann Library, 2008)

Websites

learnenglishkids.britishcouncil.org/en/fun-with-english/clean-and-green
Play this fun recycling game from the British Council.

www.recyclenow.com/schools/primary_school_resources/index.html
You can find lots of games and top tips about recycling on this website.

Index